HAPPY MEMORIAL DAY

ETHAN NEVER IMAGINED A SCHOOL PROJECT WOULD LEAD HIM ON A JOURNEY OF DISCOVERY AND PRIDE. WHEN HE LEARNS ABOUT MEMORIAL DAY, HE UNCOVERS A FAMILY SECRET THAT CHANGES EVERYTHING. WHAT HE FINDS WILL TEACH HIM THE TRUE MEANING OF HONOR AND REMEMBRANCE.

THE BIG ANNOUNCEMENT

ETHAN'S TEACHER SMILED. "CLASS, MEMORIAL DAY IS COMING UP! IT'S A TIME TO HONOR BRAVE SOLDIERS WHO PROTECTED OUR COUNTRY." ETHAN'S EYES WIDENED WITH CURIOSITY. HE HAD HEARD OF MEMORIAL DAY, BUT WHAT MADE IT SO SPECIAL?

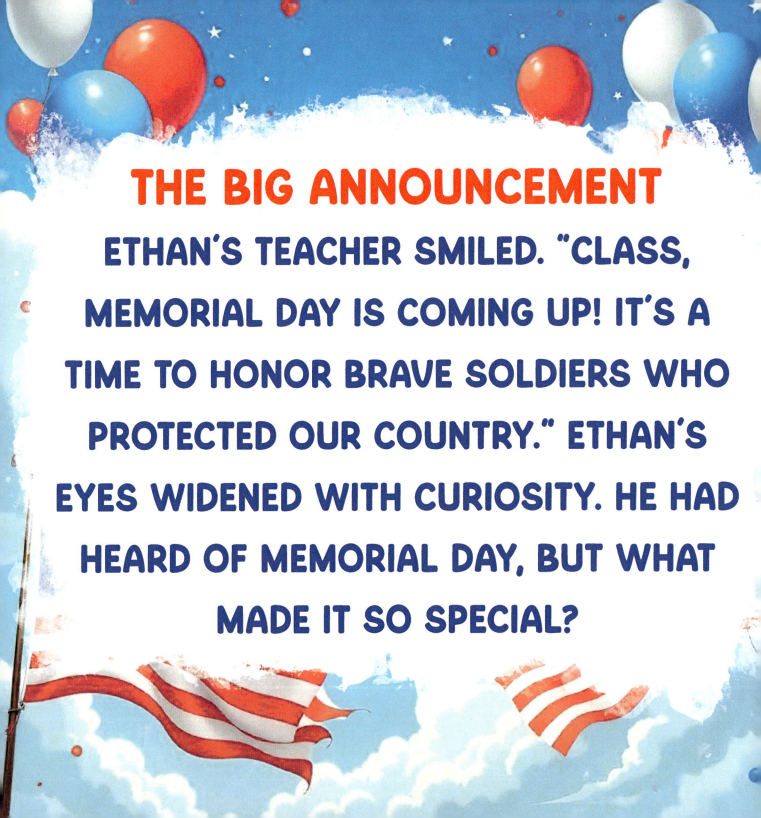

AS HIS CLASSMATES SHARED WHAT THEY KNEW, ETHAN LISTENED CLOSELY. SOME TALKED ABOUT PARADES, WHILE OTHERS MENTIONED FLAGS. BUT ETHAN WANTED TO LEARN MORE. "MAYBE ABUELA KNOWS," HE THOUGHT, ALREADY EAGER TO ASK HER.

THAT AFTERNOON, ETHAN HURRIED HOME. HE FOUND HIS GRANDMOTHER SITTING ON THE PORCH, SIPPING TEA. "ABUELA, CAN YOU TELL ME ABOUT MEMORIAL DAY?" HE ASKED. SHE SMILED WARMLY. "OH, MIJO, I HAVE A SPECIAL STORY FOR YOU."

A STORY OF BRAVERY

HIS GRANDMOTHER'S EYES TWINKLED AS SHE BEGAN. "YOUR GREAT-GREAT-GRANDFATHER WAS A SOLDIER. HE FOUGHT WITH COURAGE TO PROTECT HIS COUNTRY." ETHAN GASPED. "A SOLDIER IN OUR FAMILY?" HE HAD NEVER HEARD THIS BEFORE!

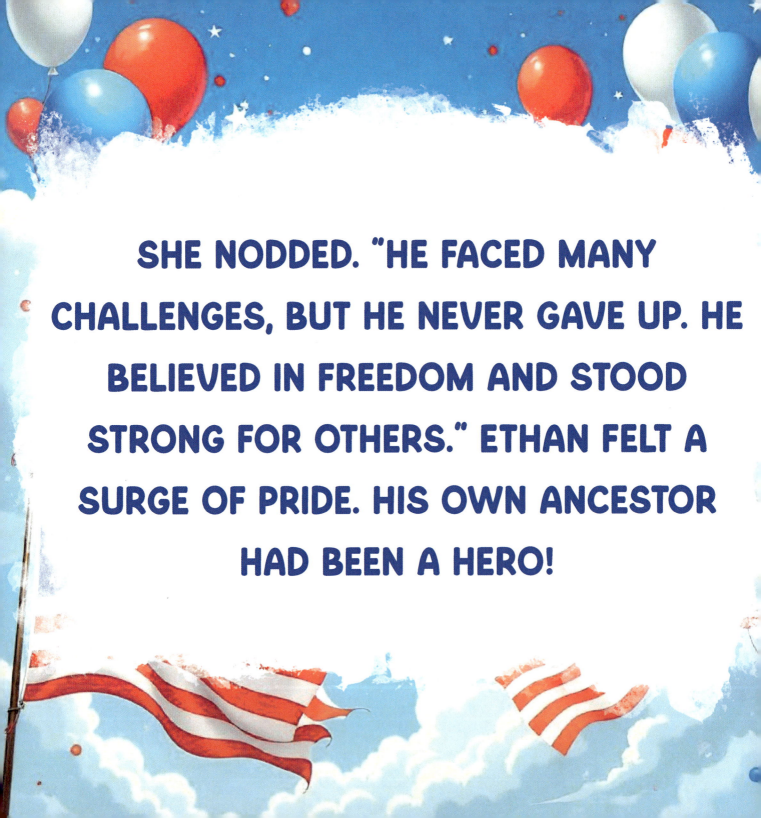

SHE NODDED. "HE FACED MANY CHALLENGES, BUT HE NEVER GAVE UP. HE BELIEVED IN FREEDOM AND STOOD STRONG FOR OTHERS." ETHAN FELT A SURGE OF PRIDE. HIS OWN ANCESTOR HAD BEEN A HERO!

AS SHE SPOKE, ETHAN IMAGINED HIS GREAT-GREAT-GRANDFATHER MARCHING BRAVELY, STANDING TALL. "HE WAS STRONG, MIJO," ABUELA SAID. "AND BECAUSE OF HEROES LIKE HIM, WE LIVE IN PEACE TODAY." ETHAN'S HEART SWELLED WITH ADMIRATION.

A NEWFOUND PRIDE

THAT NIGHT, ETHAN COULDN'T STOP THINKING ABOUT HIS GREAT-GREAT-GRANDFATHER. HE WANTED TO DO SOMETHING SPECIAL TO HONOR HIM. THEN, AN IDEA LIT UP HIS MIND. "I'LL VISIT HIS GRAVE ON MEMORIAL DAY," HE WHISPERED.

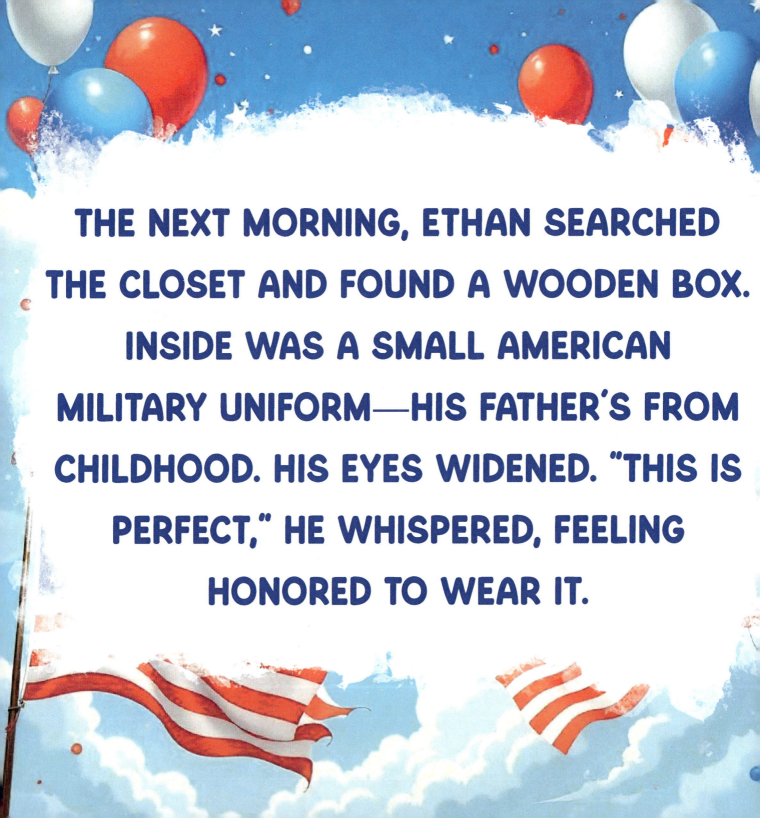

THE NEXT MORNING, ETHAN SEARCHED THE CLOSET AND FOUND A WOODEN BOX. INSIDE WAS A SMALL AMERICAN MILITARY UNIFORM—HIS FATHER'S FROM CHILDHOOD. HIS EYES WIDENED. "THIS IS PERFECT," HE WHISPERED, FEELING HONORED TO WEAR IT.

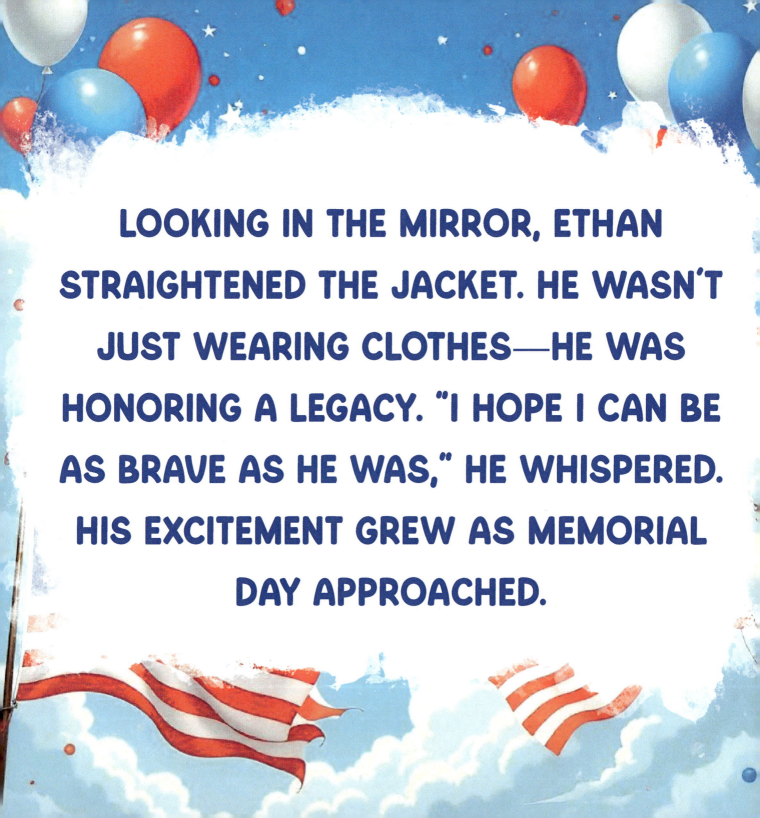

LOOKING IN THE MIRROR, ETHAN STRAIGHTENED THE JACKET. HE WASN'T JUST WEARING CLOTHES—HE WAS HONORING A LEGACY. "I HOPE I CAN BE AS BRAVE AS HE WAS," HE WHISPERED. HIS EXCITEMENT GREW AS MEMORIAL DAY APPROACHED.

A VISIT TO REMEMBER

ON MEMORIAL DAY, ETHAN AND HIS FAMILY WALKED TO THE CEMETERY. THE AIR WAS CALM, AND SMALL FLAGS WAVED IN THE BREEZE. HE CLUTCHED A TINY AMERICAN FLAG, FEELING THE IMPORTANCE OF THE MOMENT.

STANDING BEFORE HIS GREAT–GREAT–GRANDFATHER'S GRAVE, ETHAN PLACED THE FLAG BESIDE THE HEADSTONE. "THANK YOU," HE SAID SOFTLY. HIS GRANDMOTHER'S WORDS ECHOED IN HIS MIND—COURAGE, STRENGTH, AND SACRIFICE.

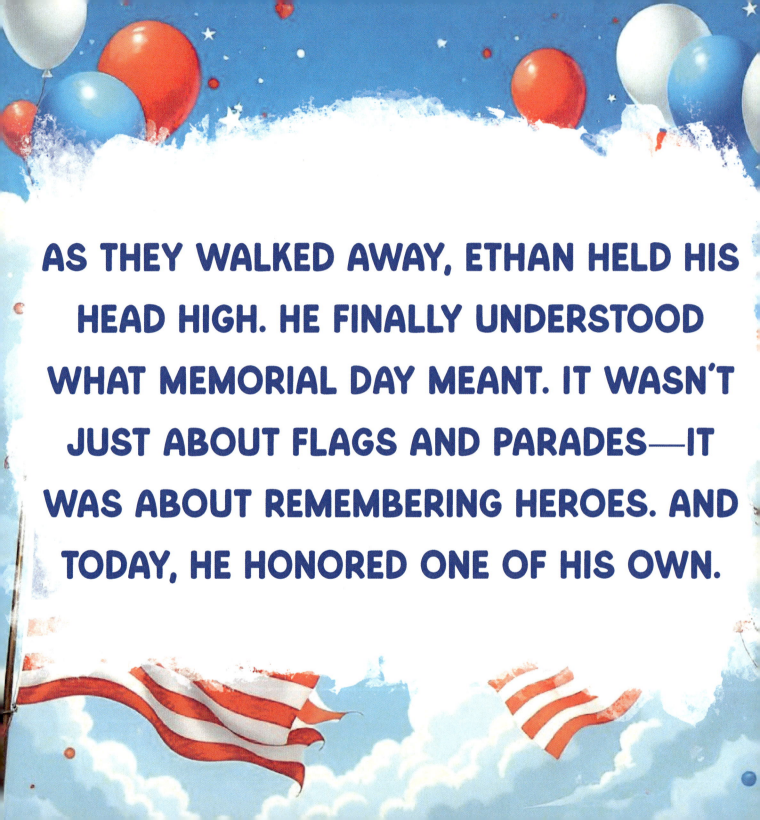

AS THEY WALKED AWAY, ETHAN HELD HIS HEAD HIGH. HE FINALLY UNDERSTOOD WHAT MEMORIAL DAY MEANT. IT WASN'T JUST ABOUT FLAGS AND PARADES—IT WAS ABOUT REMEMBERING HEROES. AND TODAY, HE HONORED ONE OF HIS OWN.

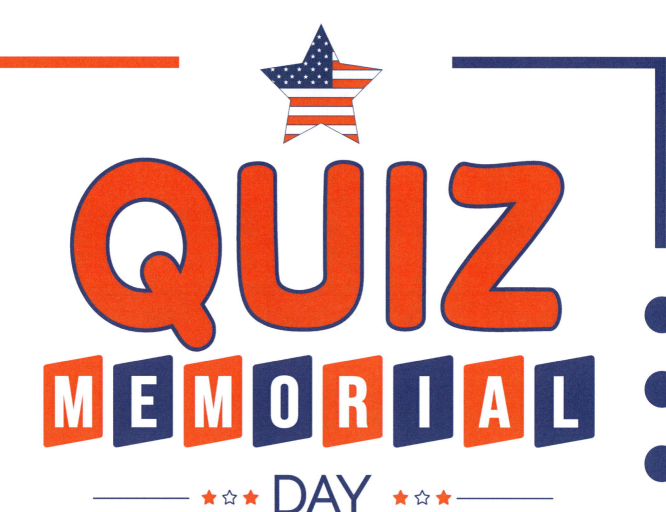

QUIZ MEMORIAL DAY

CIRCLE THE CORRECT ANSWER AND SHARE YOUR RESPONSE IN THE FEEDBACK SECTION

WHAT SPECIAL DAY WAS ETHAN'S CLASS LEARNING ABOUT?

A) VETERANS DAY

B) MEMORIAL DAY

C) INDEPENDENCE DAY

WHO TOLD ETHAN ABOUT HIS GREAT-GREAT-GRANDFATHER?

A) HIS TEACHER

B) HIS GRANDMOTHER

C) HIS BEST FRIEND

WHAT DID ETHAN FIND IN THE WOODEN BOX?

A) A TOY SOLDIER

B) A MILITARY UNIFORM

C) A FOLDED FLAG

WHERE DID ETHAN AND HIS FAMILY GO ON MEMORIAL DAY?

A) THE PARK

B) THE CEMETERY

C) THE MUSEUM

WHAT DID ETHAN LEAVE AT THE GRAVE?

A) A FLOWER

B) A SMALL FLAG

C) A PHOTO

Made in the USA
Monee, IL
18 May 2025